For Bill
with all best wishes
from Gordon

12 – 6 – 04

The
Paradise
Construction
Company

The
Paradise
Construction
Company

-

J. G. Nichols

HERLA PUBLISHING

Published by Herla Publishing
Herla is an imprint of Hesperus Press Limited
4 Rickett Street, London SW6 1RU

The Paradise Construction Company © J. G. Nichols, 2004
First published by Herla Publishing, 2004

Designed and typeset by Fraser Muggeridge
Printed in Jordan by Jordan National Press

ISBN: 1-84391-778-5

Contents

A Plain in the Land of Shinar

And there sprang a river out of Eden to water the garden...

I think of men in Shinar piling bricks
To pierce low-lying cloud. Books pile on books;
    Sophisticated scholars
Clear up obscurities with bright remarks;

Down to my daughter on the floor who tries
To make her childish letters the right size;
    Down to her frowning father
Slowly refurbishing some antique phrase –

Nostalgic for the clarity again
Of that sunshiny effortless domain
    The Source of all earth's rivers
Watered, but not for long, and not again.

Horatian

He laughs at land and lucre, gold, and even
Carved ivories imported from the East;
    And he mocks men and mazy rivers
        Chafing in channels they've chosen. Best,

According to this paragon, is: Balance,
Whatever batters you; drink modest wine;
    And - still avoiding ostentation –
        Live for the day while the day is fine.

To radiate such health when age is snowing!
To strike with unarthritic hand that lyre!
    And further, Father, in time's fulness
        Rise in the flame of the funeral fire!

Room for my Runes

Surely there should be still some modest corner
For modern priests of Helicon, who make
    A ritual of common language?
        Room for my runes with your bric-a-brac!

There are who in glass-tendrilled jars encourage
In small dark rooms the ferment of new wine,
    What fume arises channelled off through
        Twists in the system; some stick or pin

On bedsit walls with bricked-up windows posters
Fathered long since by Beardsley or Lautrec –
    Lovers of hip baths, possers, magic
        Lanterns (our delicate ironwork

Over loud shopfronts lingers from that era);
Some cultivate an accent; some long hair;
    Some hoe, trench, weed, retrench small gardens,
        Taking *au pied de la lettre* Voltaire.

The cabbage-patch I keep to is this upper
Room loud with language. Harnessed lightning here
    Breathes out less warmth than one wall painted
        Wholly with tongues, as it were with fire.

Locked up with lots of books, the most secluded
Of celebrants may yet attract a crowd
    And, happy if his crowd's a small one,
        Live with his head in a rosy cloud.

Everyone to his own Taste

Some men dream of the man they'd love to murder,
Woman rape, if the laws or God allowed it.
Some build scaffolds as high as moral standards:
    Scaffolds in Spain or

In the air, where selected malefactors
(Lesser men who are prone to lust and murder)
Swing and spin to the sound of pipes and timbrels,
    Bloody from birchrods.

Would my dreams were as innocent as theirs are!
Old age comes at my call with pipe and slippers,
Much like Milton's, dictating to my daughters
    Effortless poems,

Tough to take, but rewarding to the scholar;
Row on row of unlimited editions,
Annotated with scrupulous attention,
    Stagger the student:

Scores of subtleties pass his understanding.
What's that insolent thought from Harry Heine?
All the angels, arranged in all their orders,
    Singing of Heine?

To a Scholar

He whose life has been blessed or
    Cursed by the random Muse,
Or disturbed by a trauma
    (Call it what name you please),

Seldom shines in a bar-room
    Brawl, and on crowded streets
Never looks for his name to
    Twinkle in neon lights.

Still, when you (you're a scholar,
    Freeman of many books)
Stoop to study his poems,
    Mutter you like their looks,

Find their roots in the Romans,
    Fathom their family,
Even augur descendants
    Trained to the mystery,

Or, in fact, when you think them
    Worthy a second glance –
Then he blesses the Lady,
    Trauma, or lucky chance.

A Northern Idyll

Not for us those attractive southern landscapes
Goat-faced satyrs inhabit, hamadryads
Find so sultry they sleep around stark-naked.

Northern landscapes are bald, or, if not bald, then
Frosted over; we seldom run to satyrs;
We wrap up: the alternative is gooseflesh.

But we also – while all the uninvited
Winds gatecrash through our garden, banging bin-lids -
Rise to something that seems almost idyllic:

Reach for glasses, and fill them with Drambuie;
Roll Drambuie around our mouths, and poems
Made by men who are now more cold than we are.

Our Sundays Once

Then *Sabbath rest by Galilee*,
And melancholy hymns like that,
Made up for the Church Military
Fighting loud fights with sharp and flat...

Some weeks we'd gather in the porch
And wait to hear a baby howl.
We'd see our minister's mere touch
Wash that baby once for all...

I most indelibly retain
Hard benches in an upper room,
Hard words some corner of the brain
Hides, palled in dust till kingdom come...

The day thou gavest, Lord, is ended.
As darkness fell (*at thy behest*)
The sanguine of the sun ran blended
With terror of eternal rest...

That day about to go to glory,
My childish prayers went much like this:
'Give banal days, O Lord, and bore me;
But give the Four Last Things a miss.'

Under the Weather

Non isperate mai veder lo cielo

These bleary windows, tear-streaked by the rain!
They've been like this for days and days. No star
Will ever show its face here any more.
Do not expect to see the sky again!

We let the usual wisdom have its run:
'This gloom? Small price to pay for living where
No Fujiyamas overheat the air,
No *terremoti* turn us upside down!'

Yet still I feel uneasy when I read
Of souls I'd like to think worse off than we:
Those most despicable of Dante's dead,

Whom Virgil would not speak of but swept by,
Rejects of heaven and hell, unvisited,
Walled and whirled round by anguish and ennui.

Out of this World

There's Peel, its setting suns and slaughtered herrings,
Its castellated island just offshore,
    The tiny tilting-ground, the slender
        Tower on the island with just one door

Some eight feet up, where anxious ancient Christians
(Celtic, and so unworldly) climbed and hid,
    Hoping to live a while – their final
        Refuge and strength in a Viking raid.

There's (barren but for cromlechs) Holy Island
Where we last summer found unusual heat
    Bronzing us like Sicilian shepherds
        Casting around for a cool retreat.

With such apparent Islands of the Blessèd,
Why am I glad to be still rooted here,
    One wonders, to be warped and weathered?
        Drizzle so much of the dreary year!

Bells clanging through the fog upon the River!
Such creakings of the landing stage! Such wind
    The pilot-boat bobs hawsered! Even
        Ferries are hard put to cross and land

Voyagers venturing on a mile of water
To lose themselves all day in busy streets
    Where but two birds unknown in nature
        Rise through the mist on their metal struts.

We shuffle through the cold in sheepish clothing;
With much consideration move our chair
    Out of the draught; we ring for doctors
        Raising bacterial civil war.

That way each little kingdom seems to settle
Until revolting time insists on flight
    (Flight for, we hope, some holy island)
        Out of this world in the dead of night.

Towards the Millennium

Der zeiten flug verliert die alten namen

The year one thousand. Aachen. Widespread fear.
Wild hope of who knows what from Charlemagne.
They found him dead still, upright on his throne.
Their jaws and torches dropped. The sepulchre

Was straight resealed… So runs the chronicle.
Such scenes, or something like them, will occur
Some years from now; then everything once more
Go back to what it was, as usual.

Except for you and me. We'll feel a pang
At reaching finally three score and ten;
But then remember Adam lived too long,

And saw his language out, his distant kin
Start work on Babel. So we shall not weaken:
At least some sort of English will be spoken.

Resurrection

Reading letters we find by chance is hardly
Comme il faut; as for blowing safes apart, or
Prising open an escritoire and running
Through the contents – we know where that would land us.
Death brings changes: with *politesse* we publish
Lives and letters with crowds of little footnotes
Hissing details far better undiscussed. Just
Wait some time, and we burst the graves like resur-
Rection men, the police behind us holding
Crowds away, as we lift gold armbands, bracelets,
Bowls, and buckles, and hold them to the daylight.
I have trespassed against the dead to stare at
Twisted serpents from Sutton Hoo, stone razors
(Man first spoke, I am sure, to curse a cut), and
Odder oddments, but, most of all, one corpse (black,
Bent, and bound) in an elegant glass coffin,
Glossed by experts in gorgeous golden Gothic,
All on show, like a fish inside a tank, like,
On a hilltop exposed to wind and weather,
Snow White waiting until the Handsome Stranger
Robs her tomb, and they steal away together.

One Corner of the Earth

In '76 the two-faced month
Sees ink and paper put
To stranger uses in these rhymes
Than many will think fit.

1 When I was young my right, my writing hand
   Shook if it merely touched the corded shell.
   (I speak in shadows you must understand:
   The instrument is allegorical.
   Yet I have seen the very thing on sale;
   Last summer in Morocco I remember;
   Yes, in Tetuan, hung up above a pile
   Of long jellabas in the souk's penumbra,
   And ancient muskets chased with silver, and
   strange amber.)

2 But no more shaking now; my verses flow
   As fast as flows the Mersey where it shrinks
   Past Bootle and New Brighton, on the go
   Through channels of its sunken sandy banks.
   Hardly that flood whence Lower Egypt drinks!
   Yet what might seem a wretched stretch of water
   Over whose waste one lightship leers and winks,
   Appears to me a most expansive river,
   More gorgeous than the Ganges or the Guadalquivir.

3   True, I had half a mind to praise Morocco
    In this first canto of a three-part thing –
    Tangier, the Place de France, the Petit Socco,
    All that exotic richness – but too strong
    Proved the attraction of where I belong,
    Born as I was on the right bank of Mersey;
    Learning in Liverpool my native tongue;
    Calling a gansey what some call a jersey;
    Two syllables in Leece, and one K in Kirkby.

4   I'd love the countenance of some old Muse
    Like Clio to indulge me now and then
    As I assemble words then let them loose
    To run around my city and the men
    Who live there now or lived there once upon
    A time, that time when I was very young,
    The place where I was born – the richest strain
    Given me ever, fit for epic song.
    I'd write, *Breathe through me while I sing both loud and long!*

5   *But, clever Muse of History, abstain*
    From delving into all those mouldy scrolls
    You must preserve somewhere as in a brain –
    Dull details to delight pedantic souls!
    (Who shows each consequence of all his toils,
    And gives a chronicle from A to Z,
    Making no sharp distinction in what spoils
    He lifts up to the light, may talk us dead
    Yet leave no clear idea behind when all is said.)

6   To start *ab ovo* with the City's charter –
    Signed, sealed (and under no duress) by John
    Some years before the time of Magna Carta –
    Say where it is preserved, then on and on,
    All chronologically with each thing known
    (How Rupert's cannonade and slaving days
    Show up the enormous tedium between!)
    In my opinion is the worst of ways
    To get inside this city which I mean to praise.

7   When all around me where I walk the street
    Lie scattered relics speaking of the past –
    That shipshape hostelry, *The Baltic Fleet*;
    Goree nearby; the line of docks not least;
    Mann Island, where the buses start, was just
    Exactly what its name still makes quite clear,
    Surrounded by a forest, mast on mast;
    One roof on Wapping still says *Sailmaker*
    In fading letters for the ancient mariner.

8   To all these things there clings an atmosphere –
    As rope and tar cling in the memory –
    That, with the wet west wind and salt sea air,
    Stirs up at times in the most lubberly
    A yen to sail – as sharp necessity
    Pricked Fortunatus Wright to privateer –
    A yen to sail and sail on the wide sea,
    As though there lay, way out beyond the Bar,
    Beyond the lane of buoys, not just America…

9   How many souls, 'jousting with jeopardy',
    Buoyed only by the hope of monstrous gain,
    Have sailed those wastes of the Atlantic Sea!
    Seeking profit to more than match their pain
    How many privateers have 'ploughed the main'!
    The Mentor, so ill-built she would not sell,
    Saw Peter Baker out and home again,
    Now rich enough to raise on Mossley Hill
    The house that from his prize he called Carnatic Hall.

10 That hall has gone, where precious things were stored,
    Where safe obscurity was one time given
    To bibelots, *objets d'art*, a shining hoard
    From many lands and ages under heaven.
    There scores of model ships found a safe haven
    From high explosive through the Second War,
    And much escaped the firebombs and their ravin:
    One flowery Maytime buildings flared like straw,
    And half the City-centre perished in the fire.

11 I'd take myself – with no need for safekeeping
    Before the blast of bombs blew in our ears –
    To Town to the Museum, slowly stepping
    Towards it up a steep stone flight, eight years
    Of strict respectability, the curse
    No children unaccompanied admitted
    Feared from the dark attendants at the doors.
    Then, 'closed for the duration', it was gutted.
    For many years those steps in front stayed shrapnel-
        pitted!

12 Once past those dark attendants, I must turn
   My eyes away from two huge monoliths:
   Black as Egyptian fog, and in the frown,
   They gave bad dreams; and many regal deaths
   Lay mummied in the hall, where ancient wraiths
   Might wander were I locked inside all night;
   Old swords, old pistols gave rise to strange myths;
   Then shrunken heads are always a delight
   (Although it's hard to see how skulls can dehydrate).

13 For some years now (there should be sung *Te Deum*)
   For some years all that artistry, and more,
   Lies back where it belongs in our Museum
   Where other childish eyes, like mine before,
   Widen in wonder. But the waste of war!
   The decor is so different within:
   The entrance hall I knew before the War
   As a museum piece can still be seen
   But from a faded photograph of what has been.

14 Who though, more baleful than the bombs of Krupps,
   Who gave Carnatic Hall to death and doom?
   Who could show Horsemen of the Apocalypse
   How to hate settled streets and hearth and home?
   Look, children run indoors to see them come,
   Though walls are no protection once they're on us,
   Whose very name is fraught with glum and gloom;
   They wave briefcases and millboards like banners;
   They always call themselves (sardonically) The Planners.

15 One time the wreckers kept to Wallasey
    And plundered up and down the Leasowe shore.
    They say the vicar hollered, 'Wait for me!'
    When news came of a wreck at morning prayer;
    Flinging his cassock off into the air,
    He joined his congregation at their plunder.
    (That's in *St Hilary's of Yesteryear*.)
    The wreckers now take Liverpool asunder,
    Smash Georgian terraces, and thunder on and blunder.

16 So much that childish contemplation loved,
    So much is gone and never will return.
    Those roads where earlier generations roved
    Like bluecoat lascars milling in Park Lane!
    Those streets and squares that never come again!
    Is Gambier Terrace waiting for the blow,
    Or Percy Street, that levelled with the plain
    The ancient Overhead, and then laid low
    Goree Piazzas even, with such slight ado?

17 As once through Paradise there slid the snake,
    So now through sundry streets and subtle ways
    See Satan sliding seeking what to break.
    So Liverpool – seen most on misty days,
    Seen best when sighted through a misty daze –
    We should be glad that half your charm is hidden
    And when it's rooted out springs up to amaze
    Round corners where The Planner has not trodden;
    You have all the abandon of a tangled garden.

18 I'd like to enter here, as in a file,
   The names for somewhat longer memory
   Of everywhere that must decline and fall.
   The Paradise Construction Company
   Takes pride of place for sheer audacity;
   Little Saint Bride Street next; then Sleepers Hill;
   St Luke's, that cardboard cut-out on the sky
   Near Bold Street; the Piazza Waterfall;
   The tunnels running nowhere underneath Edge Hill.

19 Some glorious things lead nowhere. See that water,
   Buckets of sundry sizes lift, sloosh down
   And splashingly make no pretence to matter,
   Existing only to delight the Town!
   Jamaica Street stores no more sugar cane,
   But still its warehouses are worth remark.
   How often down Old Hall Street have I gone,
   Not to reach anywhere, but just to look
   Where strong wrought-iron spirals like a wisp
        of smoke.

20 That here on earth we've no abiding city
   Is still the soundest maxim ever made,
   And one we must abide by; but the pity!
   That, when all places else are null and void
   To make way for the City of our God,
   This may not be preserved, unchanged and whole,
   To show what hands most fallible once made:
   Not glittering, not gorgeous, Liverpool,
   Yet never, even in the worst of weather, dull.

Canto II

A summer of Saharan heat
Drowns in torrential rain.
Now autumn with its longer nights
Brings on my second strain.

1 We have been living more than twenty years
Over the water, out in Wallasey.
The Isle of Welshmen (i.e. foreigners)
Invading Saxons called it (cheekily),
And so called still, still not quite accurately.
For, though there always seems a wealth of wet –
The bog of Bidston Moss, the Irish Sea,
Wallasey Pool, the Mersey – all about,
It is not yet an island strictly, not yet quite.

2 (Occasionally we do have cause to wonder.
Our boundary with Birkenhead's the Pool,
And by, presumably, official blunder
There is no longer any hospital
For casualties in Wallasey at all.
What help when the swing-bridges all expand
And can't be budged, and we can't cross the Pool?
The deadly heat this summer put an end
To more than one emergency upon home ground.)

3 This almost-island then, the tip of Wirral –
   That *wyldrenesse of Wyrale* where once rode,
   After the Green Man, Gawain; where a squirrel,
   That wanted to, could go to Birkenhead
   From Chester in the south, and never tread
   The ground at all, but leap from tree to tree,
   Till Ranulph had it all disforested
   And outlaws went elsewhere – this Wallasey
   Is metalled now, and tiled, and bricked, suburbanly.

4 Though megalopolis may bear the palm,
   Benightmared in the book of Baudelaire
   Whose very mud assumes a golden gleam,
   And there are those who find fresh fields and air
   Enthralling like *la ville tentaculaire* –
   I only wish I had the skill to laud
   Our hardly-bothered-with suburbia,
   Where most for *bonhomie and belaccord*
   Mend fences, and trim lawns, and try not to be rude,

5 Which isn't easy in a world like this.
   Strange shadows stalk suburbia as well:
   There's one dark road not very far from us;
   Long, straight, and lined with sem-dets, it is dull,
   Yet not, to all appearance, terrible;
   But, when she was a little child, Elaine
   Would never go that way, but shriek and yell;
   And all of us did then, and still, incline
   To walk the long way round, companioned or alone.

6   And is it true what some historians say:
    Rock tunnels that were used for contraband
    Run all the way from Liscard to the sea?
    Most are now closed. Who knows what's underground?
    Up on this height, where there may still be found
    The old St Hilary's (a ruined tower),
    Some hundred years ago the nave was burned;
    It flickered with an alcoholic flare:
    Had liquor then been stored once and forgotten there?

7   The new St Hilary's who does not know?
    Who has not noticed on this ridge of rock
    The sandstone a mere century or so
    Has blackened and begrimed? A great landmark
    For miles around, foursquare and very dark,
    It shares with the old tower a rugged mound
    Of graves and gravestone paths. I never take
    The short cut through there but it brings to mind
    How many died at sea; how some were never found.

8   The way I talk of takes us through a lane
    So very narrow and with walls so high
    Even in summer in the blaze of noon
    It still is stony cold and shadowy.
    I went through to the graveyard recently
    And came across these cryptic words: *She gave*
    Her life for a little child. Nurse Esther E.
    Healey. Herself, it seems, she could not save.
    What, back in 1900, brought her to the grave?

9 This tomb – its sheer simplicity bewildering –
   I eased into our chatter that same eve-
   Ning, finding – heavens above! – the local children
   Already well-acquainted with the grave.
   And there were many winter tales they wove
   To clothe the stark inscription on her stone,
   Many the ways it seemed in which *she gave*
   Her life for a little child, and not a one
   But rang a deal too lurid to rely upon.

10 Their favourite legend ran that she'd been killed
   Bemauled by savage beasts (there was some notion
   That wolves in 1900 still ran wild);
   But oh the hideous ruin and combustion
   (In one account less obviously pure fiction)
   When, through the choking smoke and licking flames,
   A baby in a blanket missed destruction,
   Although his saviour smothered in the fumes…
   The other tales involved enormous seas and storms.

11 These Rachel told us whom I had assumed
   Ignorant of that screed in their own way
   So long, so well, so variously explained
   By all the district juvenility.
   Then Eileen spoke, who truly till that day
   Had never seen the stone or guessed it there;
   She interrupted happily to say
   A single word (hoping we'd question her),
   A single word, but worse than all – diphtheria.

12 I had to hark back to the bad old days
    (To hide my utter ignorance of what-
    Ever she had in mind) in words like these:
    'Our doctor always used to shine his light
    (When often as a child I "had a throat"),
    Then peer, then pause, then mutter that "in case"
    He'd "take a swab". Then we, one week to wait,
    Would pray for tonsillitis and no worse,
    And not that one of all diseases ruinous.

13 'Those days are well behind us now. Thank God
    You children never heard a doctor say
    He'd take a swab...' But they, quite undeterred:
    'You still don't tell us how she came to die.'
    Then Eileen like a flash: 'There was a way
    By which they sucked the poison from the throat –
    Before your father's time and mine I say –
    But had to spit it very quickly out.
    That would be how Nurse Healey died, I have no doubt.'

14 I might have added something, but was stayed
    In silent honour of that heroine.
    And still I'm left uncomfortably sad
    To think how Rachel came across the stone:
    She found it after walking through a lane
    Where I at least had rather she'd not stray
    Even in summer in the blaze of noon,
    So very narrow and with walls so high
    That it is always stony cold and shadowy.

15 In mind I see her standing on that mound
   Opposite Bidston and its old windmill,
   Letting her vision travel slowly round
   Beyond the Moss towards the silent Pool,
   Where all our sullen winter *Mona's Isle*,
   Manx Maid, and *Ben-My-Chree* lie lapped in peace.
   What did she make of holidays in Peel,
   Of eldritch names half Celtic and half Norse,
   Of Lonan, of Kirk Michael with its Dragon Cross?

Canto III

Freak gales this winter huff and puff:
Our fences tumble down
Who live above a littoral
The sea encroaches on.

1   How sound it is, whatever wise man said it,
    That where we drew our earliest breath of air –
    Though other towns enjoy much greater credit –
    Will always ever after be most dear,
    As from my earliest canto must appear.
    Yet we still travel hopefully. We rove.
    Two decades since to Wallasey. From there –
    Six months ago, and purely out of love
    Of change – we made within the town a second move.

2   A move nearer the sea whose billowy sheet,
    Battleship-grey and blue and dark and pale,
    Sandbanks discolour even out of sight
    (So near the surface, though the tide be full);
    A multifarious scene, enough to fill
    His thoughts who set his writing-desk behind
    The double-glazing just to watch it all.
    Long books unread, unwritten, hours on end
    I study sea upsurging in the constant wind.

3   And more, not merely water, fills the frame:
    Formby is almost obvious on the right,
    With other northern reaches I could name;
    The Isle of Man, I must admit, not quite;
    Ships often anchor in a blaze of light
    All night on our horizon; left, the coast
    Of Gwynedd leads us to a misty spot
    That's Anglesey, or Penmaenmawr at least,
    With all their mountains ranged behind them, crest on crest.

4   Our home is high up on a sort of brae
    With more than one declivity between
    Its bricken bulk and the spumescent sea:
    The broad stone terraces drop to a lawn
    (Or, put more soberly, a ground of green)
    Bushes and boles conclude to break the blast -
    No springlike Zephyr or Favonius keen
    To *re-inspire the frozen earth*, but gust
    On blustering gust, much more than willing to lambaste

5   Whatever looks it squarely in the face;
    Then there is land below, still growing wild,
    The picture of primaeval wilderness,
    I'd like to sow until the brown earth smiled
    With Latin names; next – fresh as paint, and tiled
    In russet, green, blue-green, and brilliant red –
    Some recent bungalows, a little world;
    Last swamped infrequently, more often sprayed –
    A long, wide-open, level mole or esplanade.

6   Which brings to mind another strand, a hollow
    Moan rising to a roar, another sea,
    Where glooms a silent flamen of Apollo
    And hardened heroes hassle endlessly:
    I have *The Iliad* in front of me.
    Sometimes I recollect the sights and sound
    Of Ulster in its sordid misery,
    Whose storm growls on outside this happy ground.
    I went there for a while last autumn, and I found

7   A land embattled more than might be dreamed:
    Whole districts clamped in corrugated sheets
    And tangled razor-wire, grey buildings doomed
    To stay in cages or be blown to bits,
    Wide walls left standing simply for those wits
    Who subtilise in slogan bomb and gun,
    Where *Cypress Aden Northern Island* hits
    Harder than *Lizzie is a Brit* or than
    Stone Mason will not break us, monumental pun.

8   Was *Private Shooting* unintended humour?
    No joke at all about the foot patrols –
    Four youngsters, to avoid one fatal stumer,
    Turning about like tops… And bullet holes
    Here, there, and everywhere… And, though at whiles
    A helicopter growled above Blacks Road,
    Our *Greenan* went the way of all hotels,
    Where only myths, it seems, will not explode,
    Such dragon's teeth are sown so thickly all abroad.

9   And so back home, where all the brouhaha
    Came from this wind whose hideous howl has lasted
    All winter long. We saw the sea surge near
    And clear the promenade, saw fences blasted,
    And – as by high explosive – huge slates hoisted
    Like pages fluttering from a loose-leaf file…
    But fences are back up now, concrete-posted;
    Slates re-assemble; virid spring the while
    (*Levis exsurgit zephyrus*) springs back in style.

The Forsaken Mandarin

I've seen many lordly lords
Shuffled like a pack of cards;
Some (and always the most able)
Flung across the green baize table
Just to make a dummy hand:
Someone somewhere waved a wand.

I – and I too served the state
Till I drifted out of date –
Would not wish to take to task
Anyone; I merely ask
What is left a mandarin,
In his peacock-panelled gown,
Face impassive as a gong,
Fingernails five inches long,
Hands as soft as speech should be,
Gentle as hypocrisy,
Once he's out of work and friends?

Is it time he made amends
To his *alter ego*? Mine
Is, and always was, a clown
Only happy when his speeches
Bristled with unseemly touches.
Is it time I made amends,
And that he and I were friends?
Friend, where you come frosty faces
Have to lose their airs and graces.
Since the solemn habit sticks
Come with your whole bag of tricks –

All I think I might have seen,
All I think I should have been,
Subterranean memories,
Squirming Freudian fantasies;
Gain for one discarded joker
Recognition as the maker
Nature no doubt meant him for.

Full of words I take the floor.

Belladonna

More songs than even Abelard
Invented for his Héloïse
Are sung of her, and disks are heard
In deserts and on stormy seas,

In cabins of a North Sea fleet,
In Berber tents where only camels
Look bored as ever (sheer delight
To males of all the other mammals).

Tartars have slipped upon the steppes,
Muezzins tumbled from their towers,
Merely imagining her lips
At some unseasonable hours.

In England she has left a trail
Of trembling pinstripes, and divorce,
Leaving the law to take its snail-
Like and bewigged bewildered course.

Most women still say she is plain.
Sometimes she is; but drives men crazy.
The hierarchies of France and Spain
Think more of her than of Our Lady.

They say she must be made a saint;
But, manufacturers, hold your laughter,
And think before you order paint
And tons and tons and tons of plaster.

They knew her cult in Greece and Rome:
Some poets have described quite well
How she took shape in salty foam
And drifted shorewards on a shell;

One man, to show he was impressed,
Chiselled in stone her many charms.
But what's the use? Nothing can last.
The women broke off both her arms.

2

Stop, whoever comes to shroud me!
Do not slam my coffin lid
Once you're satisfied I'm dead!
Some indulgence be allowed me!

First backcomb my hair; and then
To my cheeks' fresh pallor add
Here and there a hint of red;
Shade my eyes a bluey green;

Paint my lips a bishop's purple;
Poise my hands as if in prayer;
If my hands show wear and tear,
Aqua Manda makes them supple.

Never think me unafraid:
Be assured, my sins are reckoned.
But – too old to start a second
Life and learn a proper trade,

And quite sure no requiem
Will be sung, nor kaddish – I
In that crisis must rely
On my usual regimen.

Dare you criticise my taste?
High-toned lady, would you rather
I appeared to God your Father
All bedraggled and barefaced?

Draconian

A lady in wide sleeves and steeple hat
Stands well back from the crenellated wall,
But craning to make sure she sees it all;
Fading with age, but no less lovely for that,

Supported by a greybeard richly gowned –
Her husband (and may God preserve the pair!) –
Standing like statues, if statues could stare.
Something is happening down there on the ground.

A little knot of villagers far off
Stand ready to applaud, ready to run.
The princess, manacled, must stand alone:
For her the going's likely to be rough.

The knight – a red cross splashed across his breast,
Already horsed, and holding with hard hand
His armoured mount, the largest in the land –
Snuggles his lance more firmly in its rest.

All wait for a distant speck to grow distinct.
At last the dragon sidles into view;
Smaller than they imagined; a spark or two
Instead of sheets of flame. One shouts, 'It blinked!'

It pauses; seems to wonder what's expected.
No picadors to goad it into rage?
But obviously the knight is keen to charge,
And something of his keenness is reflected

On all the faces round, though some look puzzled.
Children recall the story was much better;
And adolescent girls begin to titter;
Till someone shouts, 'It isn't even muzzled,

'But he will fight it. Oh, the valiant fellow!'
He shuts his ventaille, and his lance is feutred.
Now all agree the knight is well-accoutred;
But what a shock to see the beast turn yellow!

It starts to scamper back across the plain,
Saint George in hot pursuit to frenzied cries
Of 'Stick it like a pig!', 'Put out its eyes!',
Or 'Head it off, and bring it back again!' –

The last too difficult for one encumbered
By tons of friendly metal. Still, the knight
Does what's expected. He does end the fight
With which his reputation's had him lumbered.

He pins the dragon like a butterfly,
But far away, which some say is a pity.
No plume of smoke as from a burning city
Signals the end, but just one little sigh.

The knight returns to music and to sport;
The people cheer him; and the banns are published.
Those nuptials mean a dynasty's established.
And no one gives the dragon another thought.

He took a part in what was no child's-play,
And music came through running through his scales;
But now he is played out nobody wails
For him… Unless I make the threnody.

And I do make it. Bring to mind a lair,
Or better if we bring to mind a nest,
The one place where the dragon's really missed,
Most when the smallest dragonette asks, 'Where

'Has Draggy gone? He said he would be back
And bring us all a beautiful princess
To get our teeth into.' To such distress
Their mother mutters anciently, 'Alack!'

A lack of what a dragon needs to thrive.
I won't repeat the victor's heartless jokes.
What wonder if his own red cross provokes
Feelings for those who don't get back alive?

Going Home

'So Galahad is back, the bloody fool!'
Such were the words which rang through Camelot.
That silent man had probably set out
One frosty morning when the tide was Yule,

Boars' heads had apples in their mouths, the hearth
Was bright with blazing logs, and men drank deep
(*Wes hal! Wes hal!*) until they sank asleep,
And carols floated on the frozen earth.

It was the custom in the great King's court
To send a hero out that time of year
To prove that knights were not afraid of fear.
He'd made the usual speech sound very curt:

'This is our certain fate: after short time
Of staring into dragons' mouths, that burn
And broil round ancient castles, to return
Into the land of legend and of dream.'

With startled maidens saved, with monsters killed,
With some outlandish areas pacified,
The heroes – always tall, blond, and blue-eyed –
Were duty-bound to come back, bags well filled

With plunder that was obvious and exotic:
Say, ogre's teeth, woodwose's head (with hair),
And endless stories of their own great flair
For various ventures more or less erotic.

But Galahad, they knew, was not like this.
He fought to win, and not to boast about it.
And as for love, he could well do without it:
Not since his mother's had he known a kiss.

Who heralded with those harsh words his coming
Was never known for sure and doesn't matter.
He was a man nobody wished to flatter,
Who'd always moved among them as if slumming,

Making his mouth an inexpressive line,
His bearing that of one who would not fail.
And now he swore he'd seen the Holy Grail –
Enormous treat reserved for him alone –

But had not thought to bring it back along!
Fancy returning with no souvenirs!
As if the fool could hope to catch men's ears,
Or rouse the poets to a rousing song,

With nothing but a haggard face to show!
To say he'd seen what no one could describe!
All that he earned was the occasional gibe
The giber took great care to mutter low.

So he will spend more days now in the saddle,
Staring into a distance that recedes,
And mutter much, but not of noble deeds;
While parents warn their children not to meddle...

The years went by till, shrunk to skin and bone,
Galahad died, and dropped beneath the daisies,
And someone made a set of cryptic phrases
And carved them for him on a little stone:

Here lieth Galahad, most sombre knight.
In all his time he made no earthly friend.
Death held no terrors for him at the end,
Who lived in darkness once he'd seen the light.

Something for Satan

From time to time it has occurred
I really ought to fling a word
(If but to show that someone cared)
    In your direction;
Yet up to now I never dared
    Address you, Satan.

You hate mankind so many ways;
You scramble all our messages;
The straightest thing a fellow says
    You bend and bevel;
And how I should address you is
    Itself the devil.

What names you go by: Lucifer
And Satan! Both names take my ear;
But both those names I really fear
    Must be discarded.
Lord of the Flies comes much more near:
    It sounds more sordid.

And what you really are escapes
All language but outlandish tropes,
You take so very many shapes:
    A raging lion;
A ruler of tomb-haunting wraiths
    For terrifying

People who chance to go astray
In Wigan or Kirk Alloway...
Even at times in Wallasey...
 Enough of this,
Which Burns brings out more cunningly
 In his *Address*.

Sometimes you batten like a leech
And – though you hardly wish to – teach
What every single mortal wretch
 Finds to his cost:
Nothing is ever worth so much
 As when it's lost.

You speak with Schlemihl, offer gold;
The deal is made, the shadow sold;
And Schlemihl smiles to see it rolled
 Up like a carpet;
And only finds he has been fooled
 Too late to stop it.

Now no more lounging in the sun;
He's naked with his shadow gone;
While you it seems have all the fun.
 What's too much troub-
Le when you're cheating anyone,
 Beelzebub?

A serpent once, you crawled, you hissed:
'Evil is good. God's prejudiced.'
But, subtler now, you don't exist,
    As germs were stronger
When they could terrorise unguessed
    At. Not much longer.

I know you're there. I've mentioned you
In several other poems. Who
Else takes the blame for what I do
    From bad to worse?
And I have had enough of you;
    And I could curse

You, poxed-up succ- and incubus
Polluting every one of us,
You never-ending stream of pus;
    And I could well –
If it were not superfluous –
    Wish you in hell.

But no curse voluble and loud,
Fit for a demon in a shroud,
The kind of curse that draws a crowd
    In city streets,
The kind mad Lear would be proud
    Of, really fits

Our charming Prince of Darkness, who's
The expert standing in our shoes,
In hipsters, parallels, or trews,
    A gentle man
Who covers with assorted lies
    Gas, baton, gun,

Who's sad that charges should explode
Before there's time to clear the road,
Who paints with word as once with woad.
    We lie and sweat
Now guilt has lost all fixed abode
    Like gelignite.

The Honours of a Feast

I write to praise not simply what we eat
(Although that subject has in it some meat),
But rather all the ritual employed
To emphasise the pleasure in a need.
Navarin printanier gives us more to chew
Who tilt our noses at the name of stew,
And some can even stomach a high bill
For burnt fishfingers, when they're *Neptune's Grill:*
The mind has its own emptiness to fill.
Mostly, I'll talk in myth. It is my taste,
And it would not become you as a guest
To say I really ought to *make it new*.
Dine elsewhere if you wish: the one or two
Who dine with me must eat what I have planned,
Not visit with a menu in their hand.
I relish myth, a sharp and seasoned dish,
Since what just happens makes a dreadful hash.

You'd think the archetypal travelled man
Would be unshockable; but, back again
In Ithaca, he's horrified to see
Food eaten in a gross, ill-mannered way.
He'd met some strange folk, and some were ill-mannered,
But only once had seen food go unhonoured –
The one-eyed monster eating meat all raw
And spitting skulls and thighbones on the floor.
Of course, it's hardly better when we dine
To find the food and atmosphere too fine.
Really, it's obvious why Calypso lost:
Nectar, ambrosia suit no human taste.

He wandered, eating well, from land to land.
The usage seldom varied. Cooked by hand,
The roasted beef, first parted from the bones,
Was munched, where possible, to harpers' tunes,
Accompanied by bread on well-scrubbed platters.
Until they've eaten, nothing really matters.
Why was he thrown up naked on their shore?
Why are his eyes still fixed upon the floor?
Why does he weep to hear of Troy being sacked?
Only when piles of bread and meat are packed
Inside him may they pause to wonder why,
And only then if he should choose to say.
O goodly vsage of those antique tymes!
Swift snacks and sandwiches are modern crimes.

A man whom fortune at the same time tossed
In the same oceans, though they never crossed,
Suffered not half so much from jealous passion
And callous gods insisting on his mission,
In terror when he passed the triple dog,
Or when his wife went missing in a fog,
Or when he lost the best man of his crew,
As when the harpies came out of the blue,
Snatched all the food away that they were able,
And, worse than that, left droppings on the table.

And that reminds me, women like their food.
A Grecian widow, famous for her speed,
Who'd sworn she'd not remarry (many asked her)
Except with somebody who could go faster,
Was soon compelled to name the happy day:
He came who did not court her fruitlessly.

Go back as far as possible, we find
That what we eat, and how, affects the mind;
So much, indeed, the whole of human fate
Was changed, and radically, by one small bite
(Some say of apple, though it smacks of quince)
Which we've been chewing over ever since.
The few perceptive Fathers all agree
Eve's prehistorical atrocity
Sprang not, as some have said, from lust or pride,
But from her too keen interest in food.
And what was then a fault is now so common
We need this fault to make us truly human.
And charity, that covers many sins,
Thrives best on hearty meals in quiet inns,
Or else at home, with gentle talk, some wine,
And nothing to be done but simply dine
And, when we get too wobbly round the knees,
Sprawl and be charitable at our ease.

Remind me, Lord, before I feed my face,
To mutter in Your ear a hasty grace.
A hasty grace. To talk till food turned cold
Would be absurd, and charity be chilled.

In Retrospect 1995

The dead edge nearer now, in the Scotch mist
That hangs so heavily round Hawthornden:
A cosy castle in an eldritch glen,
Built upon sandstone which has been crisscrossed
And strangely honeycombed, the Lord knows when,
With caves and passageways. Their purpose lost,

Or else uncertain now, they must give rise
To legends that refuse to go away.
A columbarium apparently?
A filing system? No one really knows;
And most of the suggested purposes
Serve only to provoke more mystery.

Ignoring whether Wallace and the Bruce,
And even the defeated Young Pretender,
Came here to hide (not all at once of course),
I dwell on odd events that burrow under
The surface of my mind, and have their source
In things more personal, less blood and thunder.

1. ANFIELD CEMETERY

My mother walked, I trotted, down the road
Past *Abram's Family Butcher*. The Great Gate
Drew up, as we drew near, to its full height.
Beyond it came, first, undergrowth that hid,
All but, stone slabs with just the name and date –
Prelims for the great volume of the dead –

Then more laconic burials further on,
Mere grassy mounds where no one had dug deep
Enough into his pocket for a stone,
While all agreed they should be covered up –
Who, on the parish, living near the bone,
Died as they lived – anonymous and cheap.

Once, after evening prayers and godly gloom,
As Sunday, sun, and summer died away,
A little group walked through this cemetery,
As melancholic as a fading hymn,
And poked among the graves, and giggled to see,
Mispronouncing no doubt, some Chinese name.

And it was then that George – a solemn lad
Looking, I realised later, rather like
The Saint himself taking his stand outside
Orsanmichele, Donatello's work,
With a crusader's shield and a straight look –
George thought we should not giggle at the dead.

And I knew George was right. The child I was
Found nothing in these haunts but fear and hate.
(Years later when I heard someone translate
Deus nobis haec otia fecit those
So-long-remembered words gave no delight:
'God made this – let's see – leisure, rest, repose,

This *dolce far niente* – and for us.'
It would have been much better, it really would,
If Virgil had remained above my head
With 1864, I think it was,
Over the ornate Entrance to the Dead.
So this was God's idea, this dreadful place?)

Creation was a jumble and a tip.
Little children were *blossoms in God's garden*,
Buried by Him because they *fell asleep*.
And all of us *in heavenly love abiding*
For all of this were bound to ask His pardon,
While sculptured angels turned aside to weep.

But it was *gone before* caused me most dread.
The hard wait for my brother home from school,
The usual anguish for unusual
Events, for something savoury to spread
On the sheer boredom of my daily bread,
Became a desperate longing for the dull,

Away from marble, ostentatious grief,
Dry everlastings in all sorts of weather
Under glass domes, and the de Larrinaga
Vault (like a house for sale, no sign of life,
Its doors and windows boarded up for ever),
And broken tombstones, pages torn in half.

Each night I prayed for some familiar sound –
Soft clattering of crockery below,
Loud laughter on the wireless, a brass band –
Something to make the dread of dying go.
At times it did slink off; but it was slow;
And always, every bedtime, it returned.

Yet often, after what seemed ages spent
Among the tombs, we carried on until,
Some way past Priory Road and Sleepers Hill,
We found my father standing – heaven-sent! –
Directing traffic from his pedestal
In full command of all that came and went.

And father and mother come back into mind
From this old glaucous print of *Hiawatha*;
And he is big and strong with bow in hand;
She leans towards him, smiles; they go together;
Both always setting out; until the end,
When one was left to set out for the other.

2. KESWICK

Was this in '40? Or in '41?
I well recall the place – Walton Hall Park:
A generous stretch of land for playing on,
A sort of summer-house, a boating lake,
And not much else, unless I am mistaken;
Long before my time the Hall had gone.

I liked imagining what had been once,
Now there was little left to take the eyes;
I dreamt of Babylonian terraces,
White peacocks strolling round and, stifling yawns,
Ladies conversing along gravelled ways,
With all the time in the world, and level lawns.

To tell the truth this was a barren place.
And yet we often went there after school,
While days were long enough, after the Fall
Of France. Bare earth broken by clumps of grass,
And broken also then, as I recall –
How hard a thing to say just how it was!

Imagine giant springs uncoiling there,
Left out all night until they gathered rust,
The debris of some cosmic watchmaker,
Stretching for what seemed miles across the dust,
That tore us if we touched them – even more,
That almost seemed to reach for us and clutch.

The land was broken too by lines of trenches,
And clumsy ramparts, recently thrown up.
We had been told these Iron Age defences
Were certainly the surest way to stop
Our Park becoming one more landing strip
For German gliders and invading forces.

One time – when he and I were drifting round –
The grass turned greener, even luminous;
The sky was overcast, bituminous;
Dark cloud formations looked like touching down;
And what seemed most of all most ominous,
We suddenly both knew there was no sound

And nothing moving on the earth for miles
But antiquated earthworks and wild coils
Of barbed barbaric wire from sea to sea.
Then Keswick whispered giggling, 'This might be
The end of the world.' The thought appalled; appals
Me even now. Because eventually...

That day of course we realised he was wrong.
It rained, and both of us, soaked to the bone,
Enjoyed the thunder as we ran for home.
Accustomed to a hubbub all night long
Like rattling chains and doors that went slam-bang,
We could tell thunder from the crack of doom.

Yes, it was 1940. Now I am sure.
Something I recollect dispels all doubt:
It was towards the ending of that year
A landmine on its silken parachute
Came floating gently down and bombed him out.
I know I never saw him any more.

I do believe he got away with it.
And he and all his family, I believe,
Went somewhere else – the Lake District – to live,
Where shrapnel never rattled down the street,
Where people whistled, yes, but bombs did not,
And sirens were but creatures in Greek myth.

3. GABBY ANN

I must be fair. When all is said and done
I did learn something when I went to school.
School was a place like English weather – dull
More than disastrous, always threatening rain
Except when raining, cold and miserable,
With sudden cloudbursts every now and then.

Tanks were advancing steadily enough;
Infantry followed; paras filled the air
Like dandelion seeds; but all elsewhere
And, by that stage, undoubtedly far off;
The end of the long war was very near
And, to be honest, we were all bored stiff.

In Britain in the war years we discern
A sense of oneness which is wonderful.
Historians exist to pull the wool
Of course: I must bear witness that within
That seat of learning where I set my scene
The class war went on much as usual.

Except along one former battleline.
Here the most fierce assaults had been thrown back
In seconds of the start of the campaign;
The dust had settled; we were held in check
By her we used to call, behind her back
And half in admiration, Gabby Ann.

Faced by her steady front and smouldering eyes
Our old guard even – like that famous one
In 1815 on the Mont Saint Jean –
Moved forward, hesitated, stopped, grew wise.
When those who'd not already been cut down
Took to their heels, to be cut down to size.

Only one pupil troubled her. He hit
With questions that got underneath her skin.
I hated school: he hated Gabby Ann.
'It calls exports important. Shouldn't it
Be exports are exportant, sir?' He set
Her teeth on edge like this time and again.

(Perhaps some explanation's needed here.
It was but one of that school's nasty ways
That all the women who had come in place
Of men long absent fighting in the war –
The war outside – should be addressed as sir.
So Skinner was polite. He always was.)

Finding these constant skirmishes as dull
As Geography itself, I always took
Refuge and comfort in some hidden book
To read beneath the desk. (Nothing like school
To encourage reading: one illegal look,
Those distant days, gave pleasure more than all

The gleaming volumes, classical and modern,
Studied since then. There are old men who yet –
From years of smoking where it was forbidden –
Curl one bent fist around their cigarette:
So I still tend to hold the book I am reading
Down on my lap and almost out of sight.)

I read that day of worlds more strange than Prester
John, or whatever else in Mandeville.
The blurb was over-philosophical;
Its point was put more briefly, and so better,
By Bacon, whom I only read much later:
Wild justice. But there were some tales to tell.

There were cities of refuge the Law-giver
In old age founded to take murderers in.
There was that famous monarch, the peace-lover –
His days of exile and cake-burning over –
Encouraging bloodthirsty kith and kin
Simply to take the wergild and have done.

Vendettas of the Past explained all that,
But focused mainly on the simple kill.
Moses and Alfred – neither one a fool –
Had scant success, since wreaking a complete
Revenge in those old savage times was still
A solemn duty and a special treat.

In later chapters I enjoyed my horror
At worlds such worlds away from my dull world,
Worlds where spilt blood meant more blood must be spilled:
The Molly Maguires, the Mafia, the Camorra,
The Martins and the Coys. And how I thrilled
At God's revenge on Sodom and Gomorrah!

In Iceland, with their great respect for law
And order, we find specialists who feud
All through *Njal's Saga:* Gunnar's arrows thud
Into their targets, and he asks no more;
They're safe inside their home – his aim is good –
He and his wife Hallgerd who has long hair.

The bowstring breaks. 'My dearest, cut away
Some locks of your long hair and with them plait
A new string for my bow. The enemy
Are on us now. My life depends on it.'
Hallgerd: 'You slapped my face once; just for that
I'll give no locks of hair; and you will die.'

And I read on. And read until I came
To where the hatchet-man, Skarp-Hedin, was,
Gliding with fell intent along the ice –
When Gabby Ann distracted me. Her theme,
One she seemed rather anxious to drive home,
Was the Ice Age, cold as Skarp-Hedin's face.

Plains we had heard of in the frozen north,
Or read of, or, yes, looked at on a screen,
Had once upon a time spread further south;
Indeed all Europe, where we were, had been
A single sheet of ice. A chilly plain
From one end to the other of our earth!

Time passed. The ice had melted at the edges,
The snowline moved up north, and life once more
Sprung up and flourished as it still does here.
It is as though some power beyond us grudges
That things should stay the same for ever more.
They're cyclical, of course, these great Ice Ages.

I slipped back to Skarp-Hedin, out to kill
Thrain, and still sliding on to the attack,
To be once more distracted as she spoke:
'You must remember it is cyclical,
And, given time, the snow and ice will all
Spread far down south again. It will come back.'

Then Skinner, silent up to now, broke out:
'You mean to say it's coming back again?'
'I should have thought I'd made myself quite plain.'
But Skinner had gone white, white as a sheet,
A sheet of ice. And Skinner blurted out:
'But sir, when will this happen? Tell us when.'

'Oh, very very soon,' was what she said.
And if she added, in an undertone,
'Geographically speaking', no one heard.
Skinner, now panic-stricken, stammered on:
'How can we stop it, sir?' 'From what I've said
Even you must see there's nothing to be done.'

I know that was the point when Skinner fell
Silent at last. The years have come and gone.
I recollect no more of Gabby Ann.
Along the shining ice, angry and cool,
Skarp-Hedin left Thrain dead and skated on.
I did learn something when I went to school.

* * *

Here, in this metrical repository,
Some old unhappiness is laid to rest;
As far as I can make it so, well dressed;
Composed at Hawthornden on All Souls' Day;
Like the old Castle, rising from a mist,
And like it too, half lost in history.

A Tuscan Year

Descending through the mild green Tuscan landscape,
Near Petrarch's mother's house, I've smiled to find –
   Through cypresses and silver olives –
      Find myself twisting my head around

To stare again at marble San Miniato...
I've watched the ruffled Arno, after rain,
   Rise, arch its tawny back, and foaming
      Threaten to swallow the town again...

And most, of one October, I remember
Oltrarno, in the dark, in driving rain,
   And windows lit, and fingers working
      On into evening... Now, home again,

I settle with my books beside the ocean;
The usual wind from Ireland whips it white;
   I notice ships on the horizon
      Pause in the mind when they've dropped from sight...

DEDICATION

I work from poems offered in their time
Alla brigata nobile e cortese
And meant for fellows who could take life easy.
The spendthrifts of *Inferno XXIX?*

Perhaps, though that harsh judgement isn't mine.
The crown goes to one Nicolò di Nisi
With only hawks and hounds to keep him busy
And nothing in his world to make him pine.

Folgore from the town of many towers
In celebrating such a happy lot
Climbs to the height of his poetic powers;

And I, who work with, rather than translate,
After such lapse of self-indulgent hours
Were happy to have caught him just a bit.

January

I offer, in the first month of the year,
A court to blaze with braziers all alight,
Bedrooms furnished luxuriously throughout,
Silk sheets, and scatter-rugs of squirrel fur.

Crystallised fruits fly round the board with pur-
Ple port. Such perfumes Saint Laurent puts out!
Our people have no coolness in their thought,
Though breath hangs visible in frozen air

Outside. At sundry times we pelt away,
And girls are struck with inoffensive snow,
The most exacting business of the day.

We tire at last, from so much on the go,
And watch, once back inside, the firelight play
On frozen hands and faces till they glow.

FEBRUARY

This second month stag, roebuck, and wild boar
Crowd out the forest to make up the hunt,
And friends crowd in to put us on the scent,
Than which what is there could delight us more?

Unless it be our bloodhounds on the spore.
And may you pour out money without stint,
Shaming the provident by whom it's lent,
And shaming the tightfisted even more.

We sing at evening as we start for home,
Our servants all bent double, even groaning,
Under the multiplicity of game.

Some hours of chatter, all our faces shining –
The wine is drawn, the kitchens smoke and fume –
And then to rest immobile till the morning.

MARCH

In March I see an ocean full of fish –
Fresh and saltwater – lampreys, trout, and salmon,
Dolphins, and sturgeons, and, believe me, even
The carp-like dentex, that most dainty dish.

Our sailors run their sails up at first blush
Of dawn each day to trawl towards that haven
Where you may sit and eat. This is the season
To gratify at once your lightest wish.

In chatting with the witty and the wise
In charming palaces calm waters mirror
You'll spend your day, and spend it at your ease:

No preaching priests of whom you have such horror
Mounting the pulpit with a pack of lies
(Or if they speak the truth it is in error).

April

Since it is April see the rural scene
Brighten up suddenly with song and dance,
See all the fountains playing to enhance
A pasturage more delicate and green.

See saddle-horses, chargers reared in Spain,
And people fielding fashions out of France,
So many dancing as it were Provence,
And sounding German instruments again.

And there are gardens glowing all around
Where often, stretched at ease, we see someone
Arise a little, lazily inclined

To reverence your head my crown is on –
This crown of jewels cunningly designed
To strike with awe and envy Prester John.

MAY

High time to saddle up the animals,
Ready to trot erect and apt to run,
And still responsive to the lightest rein,
Their every move melodious with bells;

Such colours broidered on such silky palls
They seem so many rainbows in the sun,
With shields painted for jousting, for sheer fun
The reign of roses and whatever else.

Now lances look to find friendly employment
And rise at length projected for mock battle,
To shudder and then shatter from the moment

They come in contact with attractive metal;
Lips run to lips for vigorous enjoyment;
And roses fall in showers and gently settle.

JUNE

Now all four *Seasons* stand undamaged where
Men rightly reconstructed, stone by stone,
Something that could not be improved upon,
The finest bridge exploded in the War.

The nearby church of Santa Trinità,
I prayed and Ghirlandaio painted in,
Is what I offer for the month of June,
And most the landscapes in the frescoes there.

Then, unimagined, in such countryside,
San Gimignano must have pride of place,
Crowded with skyscrapers, where tourists crowd

Dark narrow streets, then sudden sunny space,
And silent cloisters where cool waters slide
Refreshing the minutest blade of grass.

July

July, some time, must find us in Siena,
To follow with our eyes around the Square,
When all the course is ankle-deep in straw,
The seventeen who struggle for the banner.

We'll drink a toast, whoever is the winner,
At every banquet in the open air,
Then turn at evening to some tiny bar
To follow with *panforte* a huge dinner.

We keep the shade, while others fume and fret
At politics, the riots, market forces,
And whether the depression bottoms out.

We dwell upon the pounding of the horses,
And run a race ourselves, that is no sweat,
Around a table laid with many courses.

August

It's August. Let's go wild with thirty castles,
Each on its little hilltop in the sun.
Here stormwinds off the sea are never known.
In this mad month the very Arno sizzles.

And now and then, to exercise some muscles –
The horses' muscles – ride at dusk or dawn
From one to another, with a drink between,
Acknowledging the homage of our vassals.

The buildings blush; we feel our pulses leaping;
The most phlegmatic fails to keep his balance.
That's every day at sunset when we're shaping

Our course from San Miniato back to Florence.
Our eyes are wide with wonder, and we're hoping
For beefsteaks grilled as surely as Saint Lawrence.

No shortage of enjoyment in September.
No clouds, but crowds of pigeons in the Square
Of Santa Croce, and the first faint stir
Of something tramontana-like – a sombre

Sign, like a tiny hilltop and its timber
Behind the Holy Family. In this clear
Bright light of Italy there is a flair
In knowing where to place a smudge of umber.

Monte Senario makes us climb, but that
'S worthwhile: we taste the yellow-green liqueur,
We see the skulls of founders ranged in state

(There's one whole skeleton, a bishop's, there),
And look down on the Appennines, and wait
Even in summer for the mist to clear.

OCTOBER

October is the time to stroll around
Old Fiesole, exalted in a hollow,
And resting, like a head upon a pillow,
In what Carducci called its crescent mound.

And not in frescoes only, but all round,
High cheekbones and slant eyes! Under a halo,
Or in the living flesh dark-haired and sallow,
Etruscan features are not hard to find

Even today. Down on their plain the domes
And marble were but marsh; it was before
The rule of Rome these hills first cradled homes

And, laughter-loving as the people were –
Today we see them drinking on their tombs –
Left something mellow in the atmosphere.

November

Enjoyment's not so easy when November
Comes in with rain and masses for the dead.
Yet here in Tuscany, when all is said
And done for those we cannot but remember –

The souls of saints and sinners without number
Who stride through sunlight or are still in shade –
Then something lead-like drops from flesh and blood
And leaves it with its anguish lithe and limber.

We lean from bridges as the Arno swells,
To measure with sharp eyes the swirling water,
And shrug our shoulders when the level falls.

We hear the *bersaglieri* with some ardour
With brass and bluster celebrate All Souls:
Because the wind is chilly they blow harder.

December

The stable. Shepherds are already here.
And kings are coming in long cavalcade
On a strait path along a mountainside.
Such is the scene in Santa Trinità.

What strikes us most in this, this time of year,
Are these reminders of the world that died
That winter: codices just cast aside;
Fine fluted pillars; and sibyls in the air.

From fragmentary Latin on the tomb
And from the family in the altar-piece –
Their bags all packed for Egypt – we assume

Prognostications of such dire distress
That what is left, but pray till kingdom come?
And pray like one about to roll the dice.

ENVOI

Less simple and less sounding, I must say,
My lines than the original. I planned
My route through the remembered landscape and
With his trecento blended my today

And somehow lost Folgore on the way.
His 'crown of jewels cunningly designed'
So changed in the Oltrarno of the mind
That what is his what mine one cannot say.

And yet I have some good news for his ghost:
San Gimignano where he hung his hat
Is hardly altered from the storied past

When he and his companions crowded it
And every day was livelier than the last –
Except there is less racket in the street.

A Guide to the Gods

My theme? I think I'll take
A rather lengthy look
    At some old gods of Greece,
Gods old when I was young,
Old gods who still belong
    In any time or place.

Time was when every wood
And clearing had its god,
    Each valley and each mountain.
With all those gods around,
The man could blame, who drowned,
    The nymph of lake or fountain;

Men could have captives killed
For gods who had upheld
    The right side in a quarrel
(The side of course that won).
Some say that time has gone;
    True, tempted to be moral,

We tend to the one God,
And in Him find all good,
    Who is invisible,
Never to be described,
Certainly never bribed,
    And never trivial.

But back to bouncy gods
And goddesses. The odds,
    When poetry's the thing,
Are in, it seems, his favour
Who, on his best behaviour,
    Begins with 'Muse, now sing!'

But what did they propose
When they invoked the Muse?
    A visit from Urania?
A whip across the back?
Or merely an oblique
    Homage to their own mania?

She dwindles to a joke.
Who's left we can invoke?
    Sing Milton, Spenser, Drayton!
Sing through me anyone
Who shows how it is done!
    Sing - no, not quite sing Satan.

Why bring him into it?
This is a fiendish art:
    Do you recall that tale
Of the ventriloquist
Whose psyche knew no rest
    Because his wooden doll

Worked on him night day
While he wasted away?
      So, if I sell myself
For a devilish return,
It won't be for mere coin.
      Why should it? Books on shelf

And food inside the belly
Make more unnecessary.
      Still less for exotic learning:
The merely human brand,
That lies ready to hand,
      'S enough and more. My yearning

Is rather words at need
To couple and to breed,
      And nothing to be chancy.
And so from time to time,
As I cngage in rhyme,
      The devil takes my fancy.

But back to the main chance
As luck will have it… Once
      Upon a time there was
(All the best tales begin
In that time-honoured strain)
      A baby god called Zeus.

He was a little pest
Appropriately wet-nursed
　　By Amalthea, a goat;
Then – big and hot and bothered,
A sort of super Ovid –
　　His hobby was to dote

On ordinary women;
He even turned to crimin-
　　Al ways, as when he took
Such trouble to seduce them
Or, on request, reduce them
　　Like Semele to smoke.

Since he was not the last
To make himself a beast
　　(A serpent – swine! – or bull)
For women, we have here,
At least in metaphor,
　　The founder of a school.

Human? Yes, all too human
In his attitude to women.
　　Poor Hera, pitying him
(Bedraggled, cuckoo-shaped)
Is thanked by being raped,
　　Then married out of shame.

Again, he vents his ire
On the plagiary of fire
   Not so much by the rock
Where he chains him, or by
The terror of the sky
   Tearing with claws and beak,

As by one touch of humour:
Man, arch-eternal schemer,
   Bamboozled by a mate
Whose labyrinthine ways
Keep mankind in amaze
   Ages of endless date.

Yet all these crimes, and more,
Were meant as metaphor
   By that celestial thief,
As is succinctly shown
In *Leda and the Swan*,
   A light and low relief

On old sarcophagi
Meaning that, when we die,
   The God-Man grasps the human
And bundles us to bliss.
(And Ganymede proves this
   Is not only for women.)

His true identity?
Be warned by Semele,
    And don't demand his papers.
Dodona's sacred oak
Seems sorry now it spoke.
    And Zeus cuts no more capers.

His son who slew the Gorgon
Sleeps with the shade of Morgan
    (Victor of Panama,
Known chiefly now for rum):
Heroics do not come
    From either any more.

Only the meaning lingers
Zeus' non-existent fingers
    Expressed in fluent gold:
Love of the then Most High
Overshadowed Danäe
    And left a Lucky Child.

Strange births were all the rage
In that legendary age.
    Hephaistos' hammer thrown,
Hitting Zeus on the head,
Did not merely draw blood
    But Wisdom out, full-grown.

Face blackened in the forge,
Poor limping smith! one surge
    Of inartistic malice
(All of Olympus laughed
At him) outdid his craft:
    Mere anger fathered Pallas.

You draw what moral you please:
I have no time to pause.
    As Dante knew so well,
All fiction demands pace
(One reason why they race
    On hot sand in his hell).

He saw Brunetto run
Like one about to win
    The green cloth at Verona,
Having kept at his command
Some dignity, though damned,
    Damned, but a damned fast runner.

And, nothing if not shrewd,
Dante crowns this episode
    By making his old tutor
Turn one last time to speak
But few words: 'Read my book' -
    The everlasting writer.

And I must rush. The mighty
Most gentle Aphrodite
    Is seen best on a shell
Drifting slowly to shore.
The wrinkled ocean bore
    This fresh, uncultured pearl.

And who – seeing her thus,
Naked and nacreous,
    And wringing out her hair,
Combing it with her hands
To all the whistling winds,
    Or maybe, no less bare,

Reclined on velvet foam
As to the manner born,
    Whom waters cannot quench,
The kisses of whose mouth
Glide over lips and teeth
    Like wine – who'd ever flinch

From giving her the prize
Against Pallas, the wise
    Goddess, tamer of horses,
That very striking lady,
A little bit too ready
    To gather all her forces?

And against Hera even,
Most powerful Queen of Heaven?
    'Make love, not war,' said Paris,
Ignoring that grim couple
And giving beauty's apple
    To her who conquers Ares.

Whence came, of course, harsh war
As never known before,
    Ten years of shortages,
Anxiety at night
Worse than the fiercest fight,
    Roads packed with refugees;

While Ares' face, blood-red,
Went droning overhead.
    Yet all this seeming doom
Was Aphrodite's ploy
To make of blazing Troy
    The furnace to forge Rome.

In Botticelli's eyes
She sits, while Ares lies,
    Regarding him with pity
Whose face is full of pain
As he sleeps off the strain,
    While grinning amoretti

Play with his cast-off gear:
They lug away his spear,
    They seem to call him names,
The very smallest tries
His helmet on for size,
    And all is fun and games.

May Ares sleep so sound
As never to come round.
    Meanwhile, Mnemosyne,
Help me to make these last
Stanzas of mine the best:
    This god is good to me.

We all say liars need
Good memories. Indeed
    They do, and poets most.
Not that poets need care
To maintain the *how*, the *where*,
    As humdrum liars must,

The *who with*, and the *why*,
Lest smart alecks should cry:
    'Aha, we've caught you out!'
But they must tell a tale
We want to hear which, while
    They tell it, must sound right.

Don't think that I advise
The use of small drab lies.
     Morality forbid!
I praise large-scale depiction
Of multi-coloured fiction,
     What might, and not what did,

Occur, which needs a man
Like the Athenian,
     The expert in pig squeal,
Who got the sound just right.
I deprecate that cheat
     Who made do with a real

Pig underneath his cloak,
Hoping the truth might trick.
     Our pig impersonator
Sounded as pigs do sound
And earned applause all round;
     The while the genuine creature,

Real piggy flesh and blood
From trotters to thick head,
     Absolute swine right through,
Squealed out (perhaps from fright),
Yes, he squealed out all right,
     But as pigs seldom do.

We need good memories
To know when to dispose
    Of each bit of our plunder.
That anecdote e.g.
Which you've just heard from me
    Echoes Arany's thunder.

By now you've surely guessed
What god I've kept till last.
    Of course, the god of makers!
Hermes, of course, the bland
Patron of sleight of hand!
    Quintus Horatius Flaccus –

The hermetist from whom
I stole the following hymn –
    Stole it himself. What odds?
Who dares to look askew?
Why blame us, reader? You
    Receive the stolen goods:

Of all these gods most whimsical, most racy,
You gave, in times now well beyond our reach,
Primaeval man a prime idea of grace by
    Giving him speech;

You lend us your curved lyre, you are so kind;
You carry messages by land and sea;
And cunningly you carry off and hide
    What comes your way.

Phoebus, demanding back his stolen herd,
And putting on a face to frighten you,
Leant back in laughter when he found you had
    His quiver too.

Your help enabled Priam, heaped with gold,
To pass unseen through sharp-eyed soldiery
That with a thousand watchfires flared or smould-
    Ered close to Troy.

It must be you (who else would dare to meddle?)
Who snatch, like brands from the burning, on the side,
Whom Satan takes a hold on with such trouble,
    And safely hide.